Inside the Zoo

INSIDE THE ZOO

by Morris Weeks, Jr.

with an Introduction by
Frederick A. Ulmer, Jr.,
Curator of Mammals at
the Philadelphia Zoo

Simon and Schuster
New York

Photograph Credits:
Frontispiece, pages 19, 22-23, 26-27, 28, 34-35, 38, 40-41, 46-47,
49, 54-55, 58, 62-63, 66-67, 72-73, 76 and 95 by Douglas Faulkner;
pages 15, 69, 80, 82 and 90 by Franklin Williamson, the Philadelphia
Zoological Society.

Published by Simon and Schuster, Children's Book Division
Rockefeller Center, 630 Fifth Avenue
New York, New York 10020

First Printing

SBN 671-65117-X Trade
SBN 671-65116-1 Library
Library of Congress Catalog Card Number: 70-101894
Manufactured in the United States of America
Printed by Pearl Pressman Liberty Inc., Pennsylvania
Bound by Economy Bookbinding Corp., New Jersey

To Tony

INTRODUCTION

A trip to the zoo! What excitement and antici-
pation such an announcement used to cause when I
was a boy. Rare, indeed, is the child who doesn't feel
this way about zoos. Animals and children go hand
in hand and there are some people, like myself, who
have never outgrown their childhood fascination
with the birds and beasts. I have been fortunate
enough to work with wild animals virtually all my
life, and for me they hold an all-absorbing interest.

The Philadelphia Zoo is run by the Zoological
Society of Philadelphia which contains several thousand members. Once each year a party is held for the
members and there the director and curators enter-
tain the audience both with live animals and stories
about the problems with these creatures. And occasionally we have even taken the party-goers behind
the scenes in the Zoo. This they really love, and such
tours have quickly become the most popular attrac-
tions we ever offered.

In this book, Morris Weeks takes you "behind the scenes" at the Philadelphia Zoo. He shows you some of the many problems that arise with animals —for, being living things, they demand care and understanding and can never be treated like so much merchandise stowed in a warehouse or store. He tells you about one of our animals, an elephant named Dulary, in detail, and shows you just what is involved in taking care of her. He tells how the zoo operates and reveals the trials and tribulations, large and small, that beset even a well-run zoo. A zoo is such a vital living community that its problems are unique and nearly always refreshingly different from those of the more prosaic world of business. And that's why you will find this book such exciting reading.

You may ask a question that is frequently asked of us in this critical day and age: "Why do we need zoos?" Every zoo man is faced with this question sooner or later and, though deep inside himself he knows that zoos are extremely important assets of an enlightened society, he very often finds it difficult to come up with a simple answer.

The affinity of man for other animals is very basic. It reaches back into the dim past when cavemen took in orphaned animals—not just because

8

they needed them for food, but because they were attracted to them and wanted to care for them and rear them. In such a way did we acquire our dogs and cats, our sheep and goats, our cattle and pigs. Man even set about taming the mighty elephant.

As one leafs through the pages of history, it quickly becomes evident that zoos are no recent development. They have been with us for thousands of years and it is doubtful that a date will ever be found for the very first zoo. It could well have been founded by men of the Stone Age. But one thing is very clear—the more enlightened the civilization, the more important a part the zoo played in it. Three thousand years ago, in ancient China, the rulers maintained zoos, which were called "parks of intelligence." The Egyptian pharaohs and, later, the Roman emperors had their zoos, and such strange beasts as the tiger, the rhinoceros, the elephant, and even the giraffe were displayed at spectacles in the Roman Coliseum. From the Middle Ages down to the present time, the ruling families of Europe and other parts of the world have had their private zoos. Montezuma had a zoo well established when the Spaniards invaded Mexico in 1519.

Modern municipal zoos have had a comparatively short history. The Schönbrunn in Vienna is probably the oldest continuously operating zoo (1751). Next comes the venerable Jardin des Plantes in Paris (1793), and then the London Zoo (1828). The Philadelphia Zoo is often called "America's First Zoo," for it opened its doors to the public on July 1, 1874. Since then the development of zoos has been phenomenal, demonstrating the great interest and popularity zoos hold for the public. Today there are in the world no less than four hundred and twenty-two recognized public zoos and this does not include many small or private institutions.

Those who oppose zoos say that the animals are deprived of their freedom, and so they are. But there are other factors worth considering. A human being's idea of freedom is apt to be quite different from that of the so-called "lower animals." In the wild, animals do not have as much freedom of movement as you may think. Many species stake out sharply defined territories, out of which they dare not move for fear of attack by others of their own species. Those that do move around a great deal are usually forced to do so in order to find the food they need to survive.

Freedom in the wild also means freedom to be killed and eaten; freedom to be attacked by flies, mites, ticks, and other noxious vermin; and freedom to pick up a virulent disease organism which will cause a miserable death. And now, with the human population burgeoning, the wild creatures are literally being shoved right off the face of the earth. For many of them their only hope of survival is in zoos.

In most zoos the animals receive great care. It stands to reason that zoo people will want their charges to be healthy and happy. The proof of this is demonstrated both by longevity records, which are being broken constantly these days, and by breeding records, which indicate that those species which breed successfully are well adjusted to zoo life. Today, as their environments and diets are steadily improved, species that were once thought unbreedable are successfully producing young in captivity. The Philadelphia Zoo is proud of having the world's oldest captive gorilla, "Massa," who is 39 years old. We were the first zoo to breed the cheetah, an accomplishment that many European zoos found hard to believe when we first reported it.

As they like to say nowadays, Morris Weeks tells it like it is. When you have finished this book you will have a much better understanding of what zoos are doing and why they are doing it.

FREDERICK A. ULMER, JR.
Curator of Mammals

1

A new face appeared at the Philadelphia Zoo on a morning late in May.

It was a nice face, though you wouldn't call it exactly pretty. It rather resembled a big, gray beet—wide at the top, with a crown of coarse hair and a flapping ear at each side, narrowing at the bottom to a long, tapered nose. The nose was strong and flexible, like rubber over a steel spring. Above it a pair of brown eyes peered with shy friendliness from behind long black lashes.

Such a face, you'd say, could belong only to an elephant, and you'd be right. This elephant was a young female—in fact, just a baby. Less than a year old, she measured barely three feet high at the shoulder. A grown-up would have had to reach down to pat her. She weighed 260 pounds, which sounds like a lot for a baby—but not when it weighs 200 pounds at birth and may grow in time to four or five tons.

The baby's small ears and the hump in the

middle of her back showed that she belonged to the Asiatic elephant species. (Members of the only other species, the African, have much larger ears and a hump far back, over the hips.) And she had an Indian name, Dulary (pronounced "doo-LAH-ree"), which means "Toy."

On that first morning at the zoo, Dulary looked little and lonesome. She was alone in her pen except for a slim, cheerful young woman named Ann Lewis, who had been assigned to stay with her.

Ann was one of the hostesses in the Children's Zoo, where Dulary had been placed. This fenced-off area covers about half a city block and usually contains between 150 and 200 animals. All are the gentle sort, safe for even small children to be near. Many are domestic or farm animals such as chickens, ducks and sheep. The rest are young wild animals that may range from monkeys to lion cubs, fawns, turtles, woolly alpacas—and baby elephants.

Ann's regular job was to introduce young animals and young visitors to each other, or to oversee such special events as a child's birthday party right in the zoo with a de-scented skunk as a special guest. Now, though, she had to help Dulary get used to a strange new home halfway around the world from where she had been born.

14

Dulary, a baby Asiatic elephant, was less than a year old when she arrived at Philadelphia's Children's Zoo.

What Dulary really needed was her mother, for young elephants normally stay with their mothers until they are at least two years old, and sometimes until they are four or five. So Ann did her best to "play mama." She petted Dulary a lot. She talked to her. She let Dulary explore her hands, face and clothing with the sensitive tip of her trunk. The contact seemed to reassure the baby. Ann even put her hand in Dulary's wet, pink mouth and let her suck gently on it.

After a while the zoo gates opened for the day. Visitors began appearing at the Children's Zoo. When the first child discovered Dulary, he let out a whoop of joy. Soon other children came running, eager to see and make friends with the little newcomer. They crowded close to the wire fence around her pen, trying to reach in and touch her. And of course they offered her countless peanuts.

Dulary loved it. Suddenly she was the center of attention. She trotted around the pen, trumpeting softly, and gazed at the children with what seemed to be a big smile. Then she pushed up against the fence (which was taller than she was) and stretched her trunk over the wire for peanuts.

Ann kept a sharp watch while this was going on. She wanted to make sure that Dulary didn't hurt a child by reaching for a peanut and grasping a hand instead. And she wanted to make sure that the children didn't give Dulary anything to eat that might hurt her.

Every few hours the visitors could watch Dulary being fed. By rights she should have taken milk, but she refused it. Evidently she already considered herself too big for that. She ate a mixture of grain and chopped carrots which Ann brought to her in a pail. Dulary's trunk scooped up the food and blew it into her mouth. As soon as the food from the pail was gone, she was ready for more peanuts.

By the end of the day the zoo knew it had a new star attraction. Everyone seemed to be talking about Dulary. The newspapers ran stories about her, with pictures. People said, "That new baby elephant does sound cute. Let's go see her."

2

All this happened at the Philadelphia Zoological Garden, commonly called the Philadelphia Zoo. It is one of the more than sixty major zoos located in big and medium-sized cities across the United States. Philadelphia's zoo is the oldest of all: it was opened to the public in 1874. Today it also is one of the most important. It compares favorably with other zoos in the way it handles the main activities by which a zoo is judged: keeping a large and varied collection of animals; displaying those animals so that the public can see and enjoy them, while letting each animal live as nearly as possible as it would in the wild; furthering the study of animal health and diet, and of why animals behave as they do; finally, protecting and trying to breed the many species of animal that now are threatened with extinction in the wild. At the same time, the Philadelphia Zoo is representative of good zoos the world over in the way it is run and how it obtains and exhibits animals.

Friendly raccoons, who share a rocky grotto in the Children's Zoo with black bear cubs, love to beg tidbits of food from visitors.

The Philadelphia Zoo is not large in size. It has only 42 acres of ground. New York's Bronx Zoo, the largest zoo in area in the United States, occupies 252 acres. Several zoos, including those in Baltimore,

19

Chicago, Cleveland, Detroit, Milwaukee, Oklahoma City and Washington, D.C., cover 100 acres or more. Despite its small size, the Philadelphia Zoo attracts more than a million people every year, who come to see its many animal exhibits, to stroll along its tree-lined pathways, to admire its lawns and flowers and to eat lunch in its picnic areas.

The zoo blends old and new. Its administrative office is a small building called Solitude which was built in 1785, long before the zoo was created, by John Penn (whose grandfather William founded Pennsylvania). The building has been kept largely in its original condition, except for the addition of such modern conveniences as electric lights. An extreme contrast is the elevated monorail on which electric trains silently circle the zoo, giving up to 7,000 visitors a day a bird's-eye view of the entire grounds. Hidden away from visitors in the service area is the Penrose Research Laboratory, the first of its kind in any zoo. Here scientists oversee the health of all the zoo's residents and do important research on animal diet and disease.

Then there are the animals themselves. Philadelphia's collection of animals, one of the biggest in the country, averages about 1,600 individuals, representing more than 500 species.

The animals fall into three main groups. Most familiar to the average visitor are the mammals. These are warm-blooded, hairy animals, such as bears, giraffes, rabbits and elephants, that bear live young* and suckle them on milk. The second group is composed of the birds and includes ostriches, sparrows, ducks and parakeets. Also warm-blooded, they are feathered and lay eggs. The reptiles, such as snakes, alligators and turtles, form the third group. They are cold-blooded animals with rough or smooth skin and no covering of hair or feathers. Most of them, but not all, lay eggs. The zoo also has some amphibians—frogs, toads and salamanders, for example—on display, but no fish.

Plans for the zoo were begun before the Civil War by a group of public-spirited men who wanted their city to have a zoo that would match the already flourishing zoos of Europe. They formed the Zoological Society of Philadelphia and invited other citizens to join. Their dues, plus nonmembers' gifts, paid for the hundreds of animals that greeted the public on opening day. Among the exhibits was an Asiatic elephant—perhaps a distant relative of Dulary's.

* Except for two small, primitive Australian mammals, the echidna and the platypus. Both lay eggs—but still suckle their young.

Lucy, a female barasingha (swamp deer), is another popular animal at the Children's Zoo. Barasingha are now very rare in their native India.

The society was chartered to display animals "for the instruction and recreation of the people." That still is its basic purpose, but other things have changed in the last century.

No longer can the zoo operate just on dues and gifts. It needs all the money it raises from admission fees and the refreshment and souvenir stands inside the grounds. And although it is not owned by the city of Philadelphia, it needs and receives help from the city. Every year the city makes a grant to the zoo for running expenses. It also, from time to time, provides money for the construction of a new zoo building.

Gradually the zoo is exhibiting larger groups of fewer kinds of animals instead of just one or two representatives of a greater number of species, as was formerly the general practice. One reason for this change is that some animals breed easily in captivity. Back in 1874, lions had to be brought by ship all the way from Africa and cost about $2,000 a pair. Today almost every zoo breeds its own lions. A Philadelphia lioness named Bonnie gave birth to a litter of several cubs every year for twenty-two years, until she grew too old for motherhood. "Some years," a keeper recalls, "we almost couldn't give those cubs away."

By contrast, many animals have become steadily

24

scarcer in the wild, and some, such as cheetahs and flamingos, don't breed well in captivity. The Philadelphia Zoo may be offered such an animal from time to time, but it usually wants a breeding pair—a male and a female that have a good chance of producing young. Among the rarer species, such pairs are increasingly hard to get. Rather than exhibit a single specimen of a rarity, the zoo normally will not keep any members of that species at all.

Over the years, some species at Philadelphia have become what a restaurant owner might call "specialties of the house." One of these is cats, large and small. Philadelphia has more species of cat than any other zoo on earth. Besides its family-minded lions there are tigers, leopards, jaguars, pumas, cheetahs, lynxes, ocelots, and such rarities as the caracal, noted for its long ear tufts. The larger cats live in the carnivore house, the rest in other quarters.

Another specialty is waterfowl—the collective name for ducks, geese and swans. Philadelphia has more kinds of waterfowl than any other zoo. Generally it has well over a hundred kinds, which means there are usually several hundred individuals in residence. They live in and around a central area called Bird Lake and a series of smaller ponds laid out like stepping-stones and known as Bird Valley.

**Peter the Great, a male Siberian tiger, was born at the zoo.
The Siberian tiger is one of the animal species
which are surviving only by being bred in zoos.**

A bar-headed goose, native to Central Asia, is one of the many waterfowl to be seen on Bird Lake.

Among the zoo's waterfowl is a Hawaiian goose, or nene (pronounced "nay-nay"). The zoo is proud of helping to save this species from extinction. The grayish, black-marked bird is found in the wild in only one spot on the globe, the island of Hawaii in the mid-Pacific. It was so fiercely hunted there that by 1953 the known number of wild nenes was just thirty-three.

Fortunately, some nenes had been taken in by a British organization called the Wildfowl Trust, which maintains a kind of bird refuge in the west of England. After nenes began to breed there, a few pairs were sent to zoos. Philadelphia is one of those where the geese have continued to breed. Today there are hundreds of nenes in the world. Some have even been flown to Hawaii to restock their ancestral home.

The Philadelphia Zoo, like zoos everywhere, is playing a valuable role in the effort to save species like the nene that are threatened with extinction. Today animals in the wild are falling fast to hunters' guns and traps. Worse, they are being pushed out of their natural homes by the spread of civilization. Forests, grasslands, marshes and ocean frontage are being taken over for city growth, factories, highways and airports. Man's needs are served, but animals perish.

Today, many animal species are surviving only by being bred in zoos. Philadelphia's share of such survivors includes the long-haired, manlike orangutan, a great ape that has nearly disappeared from its native Indonesia; the wisent, or European bison, which is already extinct in the wild; the Asiatic wild cow called a banteng; the Siberian tiger; the Malayan tapir; and North America's trumpeter swan, largest and rarest of all swans.

Philadelphia has bred a variety of other mammals and birds too—giraffes, polar bears, kangaroos, cheetahs, camels, black jaguars, flamingos, ibises, steamer ducks and many more. In a number of cases it was the first zoo to breed these animals. Its breeding successes have helped to maintain its own collection and those of other zoos.

What about Dulary? Was she bred at the zoo?

No. The elephant is one animal that is never bred at Philadelphia. With the notable exception of the municipal zoo in Portland, Oregon, where several baby elephants have been born just in the last few years, elephants are rarely bred in any zoo. The reason is that while zoo life suits most female elephants, it makes most males hard to handle and even dangerous to their keepers. Few zoos even exhibit males.

3

Wherever they come from, new faces appear at zoos more often than you might think. Animals, like people, get hurt or fall sick and die. To keep up the collection, replacements are needed regularly. The Philadelphia Zoo loses about ten percent of its animals—more than 150 mammals, birds and reptiles—every year. Usually they are replaced as soon as possible.

Dulary herself was a replacement, though an unusual one. The zoo had a baby elephant named Nang Chang that was a great favorite with Philadelphians. When she died in an accident, many children were saddened. The zoo naturally wanted to replace her, but it didn't have the money.

Money is almost always a problem for zoos. Even a city-owned zoo is limited in what it can spend, and must prepare a careful annual budget—an estimate of its financial needs for a whole year—and hope it will receive as much money as it needs. A private zoo like Philadelphia's has to be even more careful.

The Philadelphia budget is drawn up by the zoo's professional staff and is then presented to the board of directors of the Zoological Society, who must approve it. It now comes to more than $1,000,000 a year. This is a lot of money, but it has to cover a lot of expenses.

The biggest expense is salaries. The zoo employs about two hundred people, who work five days a week, the year around. In addition, there are such employees as the Children's Zoo hostesses, who are hired only for the summer months when the area is open. The most important individual employee is the director. He is in charge of running the zoo, with the Zoological Society's approval. The most numerous employees are the maintenance men, who keep the buildings and grounds in good shape, and the catering staff, who operate the refreshment stands and the employees' lunchroom.

The director has three top assistants, the curators. Each one is responsible for one of the three big animal collections (mammals, birds, reptiles). Each curator keeps records of all the arrivals, departures, births and deaths in his animal collection. He plans the acquisition and display of new animals. And he supervises the keepers, who actually take care of the animals.

The Philadelphia staff includes some forty keepers, headed by the Superintendent of Animals and three head keepers (one for each collection). Every keeper has his own duties. Here is what those are for a keeper we'll call Jim:

Jim looks after two groups of animals in different parts of the zoo. One group normally includes five zebras, two onagers (or wild asses) and five camels. The other group includes all the zoo's canines (dog-like animals)—usually, about fifteen wolves, five foxes, two coyotes and an assortment of other animals that changes from time to time.

Jim's day starts at eight in the morning. His first chore is to hose down all the cages in the canine area. Then he inspects all his charges to see if there is any change in their condition since the day before—illness, an injury, an unexpected birth and so on. He reports his findings to the Head Keeper of Mammals. Then he cleans out the enclosures of the hoofed animals and gives each one enough hay to last it for twenty-four hours. Then it is time for Jim to have lunch, which he may bring from home or buy in the zoo lunchroom.

Jim gives the hoofed animals a feeding of grain

33

Hundreds of thousands of children come to the zoo each year to see the live animals. Those made of stone are popular too.

in the afternoon. Then he moves to the canine area and gives the occupants their one meal of the day—a mixture of prepared food (not unlike canned dog food) with added minerals and vitamins. He carries the mixture in a pail and tosses it by hand to each animal, making sure that all get enough.

There may also be "housekeeping" to do. For example, a drain in the water trough of the zebra enclosure may have become clogged with chewed-up hay, dribbled in when the animals drink. The keeper clears out the pipeline just as a plumber might clear out your mother's stopped-up kitchen sink.

Jim's day ends at five in the afternoon. He works a five-day week. Because the zoo is open every day of the year (except Thanksgiving, Christmas and New Year's Day), keepers' work weeks are staggered so that some keepers work weekends and there is always a full crew on duty.

In days past, most keepers were men who had grown up on farms or had worked in circuses and thus were familiar with animals when they started working for the zoo. Today they may come from anywhere, and a few of them are women. The main requirement for the job is the ability to get along with animals and to enjoy the daily labor of taking care of them.

Curators, by contrast, are usually trained scientists who haven't necessarily had much experience in working directly with animals. Most of them majored in zoology (the study of animals) at college and stay closely in touch with that field of knowledge. They write articles for scientific journals, attend meetings of scientists and sometimes teach zoology or a related subject at a university.

Because of a generally deserved reputation as authorities about the animals in their charge, the curators also serve as a contact between the zoo and the public. Whenever someone in the Philadelphia area has a question about an animal, it is usually the curator who answers it.

"I get up to a hundred and fifty telephone calls a week—plus letters," says Curator of Mammals Frederick A. Ulmer, Jr. "Most people ask about feeding or caring for a wild pet. I try to advise them simply and clearly. Then there are people who took in some animal and now want to get rid of it. They often offer it to the zoo, but I almost always have to refuse. More people seem to have raccoons and monkeys than any other mammal. Unfortunately, the zoo rarely needs these run-of-the-mill creatures.

"Sometimes there are exceptions. Someone offered the Indianapolis Zoo what seemed like an un-

Curator of Mammals Fred Ulmer has raised many zoo animals at home. Here he is seen with Lucy, whom he raised on a baby bottle.

usual ape. The zoo sent me a photo and asked my opinion. I told them it must be a pygmy chimpanzee, a real rarity. That was one gift they didn't refuse."

Besides salaries, the Philadelphia Zoo's main

expenses include operating costs (such as electricity and telephone service), building repairs and maintenance, animal feed, materials and equipment for the laboratory—and the acquisition of animals. This last is a relatively small part of the regular budget.

One reason is that many animals can be obtained without cost. Some animals, as we have seen, are born right in the zoo. Some are received in trade from other zoos—a porcupine for a pair of ducks, a stork for a gazelle. Zoos send out lists of what they are looking for and what they can offer in exchange. Sometimes two zoos create a breeding pair, using one mate from each zoo.

"We did that with the Baltimore Zoo," Frederick Ulmer remembers. "They had a male of a rare species, the pygmy hippopotamus, and we had a female. We sent two keepers in a truck to Baltimore to bring back the male, then introduced him to our young lady and left them alone.

"In due time they had a healthy baby. It stayed here with the mother. But next time, if there's another, Baltimore gets it."

Other free animals include the occasional gift and the even more occasional stray, such as a migrating goose separated from its flock. But none of these can be counted on just when a replacement is needed.

Rango, a male Sumatran orangutan, is very mischievous when he is not asleep. He keeps breaking all his play equipment.

Particularly when the zoo needs the more expensive animals, such as elephants, it almost always has to spend money.

Philadelphia's budget does allow a certain amount of money each year for purchasing new animals. Curators may spend what they need for goats, otters, pheasants, rattlesnakes and other such ordinary replacements. But some aren't ordinary. Rare animals keep getting more expensive. A mountain gorilla can cost more than $12,000; a shoe-billed stork, close to $2,000; the exceedingly scarce white rhinoceros, as much as $25,000.

For such expenses the zoo must take special measures. It may appeal to a rich friend. It may put on a drive to raise money from the general public. It may take funds set aside for something that can be postponed, such as a new roof for the Monkey House, and spend them on a single animal that it badly wants.

When the Philadelphia Zoo was looking for a replacement for Nang Chang, a new baby elephant cost about $3,000. The zoo director was wondering just how he could find this much money when a friend of the zoo telephoned to say that he had read of Nang Chang's death and wanted to pay for a replacement. His offer was accepted gladly. Soon an announcement went out: "Hundreds of thousands of children who will visit the zoo next year will not be disappointed. There will be another baby elephant to greet them."

That still left the question: Where would the zoo get her?

4

Years ago, when a zoo wanted new animals, it often sent out an expedition to capture them. Men experienced in rounding up large animals or trapping smaller ones would go by ship to Asia, Australia, Africa or South America. They would hire natives to help them and strike out into the wild country where the animals lived. They would stay as long as necessary, sometimes many months, to catch what the zoo wanted. Some zoos, including Philadelphia's, kept an animal collector on the staff and sent him off regularly.

The captured animals were given the best possible care, but that often wasn't good enough. Some died for lack of the right food, or from disease, or because they got to fighting and one killed another. Still more might perish during the long voyage home. Finally, those that survived were placed on exhibition.

Today such collecting trips are uncommon (although the Baltimore Zoo got its male pygmy hippo by sending an expedition to Liberia, in West Africa). There are two main reasons:

First, the trips have become too expensive for what they produce. Apart from the costs of travel and shipping, most desirable wild animals have diminished in numbers. They are harder to locate, and this is expensive. Many countries now require a collector to buy a special license for some kinds of animals. Some species may not be taken at all.

Second, zoos have developed other ways of obtaining new animals, such as breeding or trading. And frequently they obtain animals through an animal dealer who, typically, does business with many zoos.

An animal dealer has contacts in areas where animals still may be collected and has a sharp eye for both supply and demand. He knows whom to call on —or, if necessary, where to go himself—when a zoo wants, say, a fleet-footed impala from East Africa or a furry binturong from the East Indies. Some dealers specialize in animals from just one area or of just one kind, such as sea lions.

Many dealers advertise in publications put out for zoo men. An advertisement may say that a dealer "has" an animal; that means he knows someone who

**Golden Girl and Golden Boy,
rare Great Indian one-horned rhinoceroses,
were captured in the Kaziranga Sanctuary in Assam, India.**

has captured it and will hold it for the dealer until a buyer is found. If the ad says the dealer "can get" the animal, it means he knows where one has at least been spotted and is willing to go after it if a zoo offers him a fair price.

Wild animals today are caught in various ways, depending on their size and habits. Such speedsters as antelopes and giraffes may be run down on the open plains by men driving trucks and carrying lassos. A strong, well-armed creature like a gorilla generally is "shot" with a dart containing an anesthetic that puts it to sleep long enough for it to be tied up. A tiger or leopard also may be "shot," or may be trapped in any of a variety of ways.

A noose on a stick is used with most poisonous snakes, and it can also be used to catch an alligator by the jaws. Flying birds are commonly taken with birdlime—a sticky substance that holds their feet to a branch where they alight to feed—or in a light but strong net called a mist net, placed in an opening through which the birds often fly. Larger birds may be lassoed. Smaller mammals and reptiles may be caught in simple traps.

Today, anyone going after wild animals for zoos makes every effort to capture and keep them in good physical condition. And the animals (even fish) gen-

An elevated monorail takes visitors all around the zoo grounds.

erally are flown directly from where they are caught to where they will be exhibited.

When a zoo receives an animal, it normally has the right to hold the animal for a day or two to observe its health and behavior. If these are not satis-factory, the animal can be rejected and the dealer gets no pay.

So it was with Dulary. When the Philadelphia Zoo was ready to buy a baby elephant, Frederick Ulmer got in touch with an animal dealer in New York City and described the kind of animal he wanted. He said it should be delivered in May, when the weather was warm enough for zoo animals to be outdooors but before the rush of summer visitors. The dealer agreed to do his best.

One day he telephoned and said, "I've got your baby!"

Since dealers don't like to reveal their contacts, the exact way this dealer found Dulary is his secret. The zoo does know that she started life in Thailand, in southeastern Asia. People in that jungle region have used elephants for centuries as work animals. Since they are very strong and not too hard to train, elephants are good for such heavy jobs as hauling teakwood logs through country where there are no roads. In any herd of work elephants, babies are born. Dulary may have been such a baby.

Or Dulary and her mother may have been caught together in a *keddah* drive. That means a roundup of wild elephants—adults that can be trained to work and babies that can be sold. In India, where work elephants also are used, the law will not let a native-born elephant be taken out of the country until it is at least four feet tall (meaning more than a year old). But Thailand had no such law when Dulary was born, so she left her homeland early.

Dulary traveled westward by way of India (where she probably received her name) to the city of Osnabrück in West Germany; for some reason, the dealer wanted to give her a temporary home until he was ready to have her crated and put on an airplane for the United States. She stayed in Osnabrück only six weeks, but that was long enough to make her popular. When she arrived in Philadelphia, a letter from Osnabrück arrived too. It said that the German zoo had been feeding her mainly milk, bread and fruit—and that the children of Osnabrück wished her a long, happy life in America.

5

When Dulary arrived at Kennedy International Airport in New York City, she was met by Frederick Ulmer and a keeper, who had driven a zoo truck to New York from Philadelphia. They found Dulary none the worse for her solitary ride across the Atlantic Ocean. They gave her some bananas and had the crate loaded onto the truck. Then they went to dinner, leaving the truck at an animal shelter in the airport.

While they were gone, Dulary somehow got the door of her crate open and decided she would have dinner too. Spotting more bananas in a nearby box, she gobbled up a couple of dozen before the men came back. It might have been more if a shelter attendant hadn't heard her and coaxed her back into the crate. Her introduction to America might have been an elephant-sized stomachache.

It was late when Dulary's crate was unloaded at Philadelphia's Children's Zoo. She spent the rest of the night in a barn there, but not alone. Norman Hess, the Head Keeper of Mammals, felt that the little stranger might be lonely and anxious—so he slept with her.

"I woke up every so often," he says, "to eye the clock and listen for sounds of an unhappy elephant. But Dulary never whimpered. I guess she's just naturally good-natured." In the morning Dulary began her new life as a crowd pleaser. She had been in the United States less than a full day.

Not all zoo animals go on display as quickly as that, for various reasons. Many of them must first pass through quarantine—an isolated area, away from other animals, where they can be watched to make sure they are healthy.

Certain kinds of animals may carry diseases that other animals could catch. Hoofed mammals—deer, antelope, buffalo, giraffes and others—can have foot-and-mouth disease or rinderpest, both very dangerous to cattle (wild and domestic) and somewhat so to sheep and pigs. Zebras, onagers and other equids (horselike animals) may have ailments that horses could catch. Parrots may carry psittacosis, a threat to apes and humans as well as to all the other parrot-like birds, of which no fewer than 315 species are known.

**This giant tortoise comes from
the Galapagos Islands in the Pacific Ocean.**

Hoofed mammals and such birds as pheasants, quail, ducks, geese and swans that are headed for American zoos must, by law, spend up to two months at the U.S. Department of Agriculture's quarantine station in Clifton, New Jersey. Each animal is tested for disease when it arrives, then watched carefully to see whether it develops any symptoms. Only when the veterinarians (animal doctors) at the station are positive that the animal is disease-free do they release it to the waiting zoo.

Most zoos also have their own quarantine areas for animals that might infect others or might be sick themselves. Practically any animal may have body parasites—fleas or mites on the skin, for example, or worms in the intestines. Parasites can weaken an animal to the point of exhaustion. In former years they actually killed hundreds of zoo dwellers. Today parasites are controlled during the quarantine stay by antibiotics and other drugs which are given by injection or mixed with the animals' food.

Then there are diseases peculiar to one creature or another. Wild canines may get distemper just like domestic dogs, and are protected against it with the same vaccine used on pet poodles. A different type of distemper infects the wild cats and is controlled by a domestic-tabby vaccine. Apes and monkeys may develop pneumonia, tuberculosis and other ailments familiar to man, including colds. As a Philadelphia scientist puts it: "Just about anything you can get, an ape can."

To safeguard the zoo's own animals, the Penrose laboratory was a pioneer in working out a reliable test for tuberculosis in apes and monkeys. Today the zoo quarantines them for up to six months. When they go on display, they are kept well away from contact with possible germ-carrying visitors.

Elephants, luckily, get very few ills that can be transmitted to other animals. Thus they usually bypass quarantine and go on display as soon as the zoo is sure they are healthy. With Dulary there was no question about that.

But health is not the only thing to be considered when a new face appears in the zoo. Some animals react violently when they are let loose in strange surroundings. The unfamiliar sights and smells can make them extremely nervous, even panicky. Hoofed animals such as deer and antelope have been known to dash blindly into fences or walls, breaking their legs or even their necks. Keepers are always relieved when this period of wild fear ends.

Then there is the problem of animals that normally live in a herd or pack. These include most

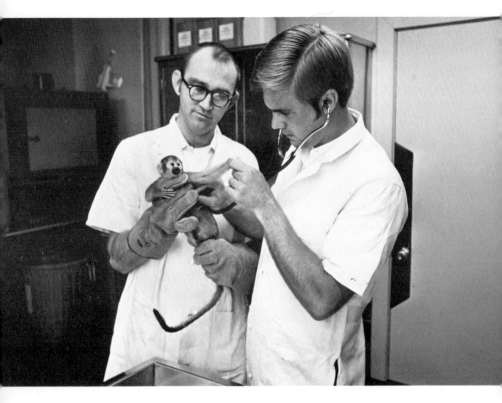

At Penrose Research Laboratory, Dr. Kevin Fox holds a squirrel monkey while veterinary student Joseph Tuckosh checks its heart rate and respiration.

hoofed mammals, wolves, many kinds of monkeys, various rodents and many birds.

When one of these animals is put in with a zoo group, all the "old settlers" spot him as a newcomer.

58

Any or all of them may attack him, one at a time, not to kill or even hurt him but to establish who is boss. Each individual fight continues until one animal breaks off and moves away, leaving the other in the boss position. If the newcomer is timid or weak, he may wind up being bossed by all the others. Sometimes he is so tough that he wins his way to leadership of them all. But until this important matter is settled the newcomer cannot be accepted as one of the group.

A special problem can come up when animals of different species are put in the same enclosure and one kind attacks the other. This has happened with, for example, two species of antelope: the large, almost cowlike eland and the lesser kudu, which is smaller and lighter. Together, the two make a more interesting exhibit than either would alone—but not if the male eland charges the male kudu on sight and makes him too jittery to eat.

How would you solve that problem? One German zoo found an answer. A small artificial hill was raised in the center of the enclosure, so that the eland normally wouldn't see the kudu and therefore would let him alone. "Out of sight, out of mind."

6

None of these problems occurred with Dulary. She didn't panic in her new home. Elephants are herd animals, but Dulary was far too little to be put in with the zoo's two full-grown females, Peggy (a big Asiatic) and Petal (a slightly smaller African). Instead, Dulary had a pen all to herself and an attendant who quickly grew very fond of her.

"I liked Dulary from the first day," Ann Lewis says. "Maybe it was because she did need me. I worked hard at being a mama to her, and you could tell she was grateful.

"I began coming in early every morning to fix her food for the day. As soon as she saw me, her ears stood out like a couple of little sails and she started to trumpet. Then she trotted up to me like a pet dog.

"And eat! She gained fifty pounds the first week!

"Then she started to lose a little, so we changed her diet. We put her on the laboratory's special formula."

That formula is a story in itself. Originally, the zoo tried to feed every animal what it had been used to in the wild, or at least something roughly like it. Many zoos still try to do this.

But the Penrose laboratory decided it was impossible to match hundreds of different natural diets. Thus there was no way to be sure each animal got the nourishment it needed. So the laboratory people did some careful studies of animal nutrition and gradually figured out a basic formula for each main kind of animal. All the formulas could be prepared right in the zoo from readily available foods, at reasonable cost, in whatever amounts might be needed.

The formulas don't make exciting reading, but they certainly are scientific. Take Diet A, for omnivorous mammals and birds—those that normally eat meat, vegetables and just about everything else. It consists of ground yellow corn, ground whole wheat, ground whole barley, ground rolled oats, peanut meal, soybean meal, alfalfa-leaf meal, dried skim milk, oystershell flour, iodized salt and vitamins, all mixed with ground boiled meat and water to make what in Philadelphia they call zoo cake. "You could eat it yourself!" one keeper says. In any case, it has proved to be a good and complete food for apes, monkeys, bears (when a few ingredients are added),

Ann Lewis holds two baby gorillas, recent arrivals from Holland. Their native home is West Africa.

rodents, wild pigs and, of all things, the two-toed sloth. It also nourishes most waterfowl, cranes, doves, grouse, pheasants, ostriches, flamingos and the great majority of parrots.

Diet B, a somewhat different formula, does the job for herbivores—the mammals that live only on vegetable matter. Animals that thrive on Diet B include wild cows and horses, deer, antelope, giraffes, hippopotamuses, rhinoceroses, camels, buffalo and kangaroos.

Diet C, which consists basically of ground raw meat plus minerals and vitamins, goes to most carnivores—such mammals as canines, weasels and raccoons; such birds as crows, owls, eagles, hawks, vultures; and a variety of reptiles. The cats get a similar diet, but their raw meat isn't ground up because they need the exercise of tearing it up with their teeth.

The only animals for which no special diet has been found are the fish eaters—sea lions, penguins, pelicans and the like. The zoo simply feeds them fish, bought from dealers. "We have found no practical method," a laboratory bulletin gravely states, "by which fish may be improved."

The basic diets have been modified in special cases. One rather spectacular trick was adding carrot

64

juice to Diet A when it was fed to flamingos. In nature, the flamingos' plumage glows with shades of red, pink and orange, but in zoos it may lose its color unless that touch of carrot is there. Another diet is for anteaters. In the wild they live almost exclusively on ants, but the zoo keeps them thriving on canned dog food, milk, ground meat, a helping of Diet A, peanut oil and vitamins.

As for Dulary, *her* special formula was based on a diet first created for sick monkeys. It consisted mainly of commercial baby cereal and powdered milk. To this were added rolled oats, raisins, corn syrup and bananas. Ann fed the mixture to Dulary four times a day all through the little elephant's first summer. By September she weighed about 500 pounds, twice as much as she had when she arrived in May.

Dulary was weighed once a week that season. The zoo has a big scale for its trucks in the service area, and Ann soon found she could walk Dulary there and right onto the scale. The two of them would head out into the "big zoo" in late afternoon. As they moved along, grown-ups stared and boys and girls hurried up to watch and to pat Dulary as she passed.

Ann always put a collar around Dulary's neck.

Pierre, a young male African lion, was born in a zoo in Dallas, Texas. He came to Philadelphia when he was three months old.

She carried a prod (a wooden staff with a metal tip) in case she had to restrain her charge. But Dulary never even tried to break away. She had accepted Ann as a foster mother and followed dutifully wherever Ann went. These afternoon strolls became a daily event, and Dulary awaited them as eagerly as she did Ann's appearance in the morning.

Just once did a little trouble erupt. On Ann's day off, two experienced zoo men, the Superintendent of the Children's Zoo and the Head Keeper of Mammals, tried to take Dulary for her stroll. She liked them both, but she wasn't used to following them around. So Dulary decided to set off on her own. She suddenly broke into a trot, and one man lost his hold on her. Then she charged happily through a hedge outside the birdhouse, and the other man was swept aside. The house itself stopped her until the two panting, red-faced escorts could catch up.

When not out walking, Dulary was quite content in her pen. Like many Asiatic elephants, she liked bathing, so a shower and wading pool were built for her. She enjoyed them especially on hot days. Sometimes Ann took off her shoes and socks and waded too.

"Dulary just loved company," she says. "If I sat down in her pen to rest, she might amble over and

Like many Asiatic elephants, Dulary likes to bathe.

stand so close that she was almost touching me. She always placed those big round feet of hers very carefully, so I wouldn't be stepped on. I think she would have gotten onto my lap if I'd let her. But the risk of being squashed flat was too great.

"Imagine that—a lap elephant!"

By mid-October, Dulary had been visited and admired by thousands of boys and girls and nearly as many grown-ups. Then the Children's Zoo closed for the season and the hostesses left. But Ann stayed. She had decided to continue with zoo work as a keeper, and the zoo was glad to hire her. After Dulary was put in the barn for the winter—the same barn where she had spent her first night—Ann continued to come every day to feed and pet her and, if the weather was nice, to take her outside.

In the spring the Children's Zoo reopened for another season. Again Dulary was its star, with Ann her faithful attendant. Dulary was growing all the time. She weighed almost 1,000 pounds. But she still was a baby, in elephant terms, and someone always had to keep an eye on her when visitors pressed close and possible danger arose. Generally, that someone was Ann.

7

Suddenly it was October again. The trees in the zoo were turning red and gold, and brown leaves piled up on walks and lawns. The sun was warm at noon but the nights were getting chilly. The Children's Zoo closed for the winter. This fall Dulary was not put in the barn. Instead, she entered a whole new world—the Elephant House, where the full-grown Peggy and Petal were tended by a male keeper.

The big elephants had been in the zoo for years. Each had her own cage in the Elephant House, a handsome building with stone walls and a sloping roof. Other enclosures sheltered the zoo's rhinos and hippos. All the animals had outside areas, separated from the public by moats and fences, where they could roam about in good weather. The moat was narrow enough for an elephant to stretch its trunk across when peanuts were offered.

Inside the house was a long gallery along which visitors could walk to see all the animals on rainy

Jimmy, a male hippopotamus from tropical Africa, is one of the zoo's oldest animals and the father of many babies.

days or in cold weather. Each of the elephant cages had steel bars on the visitors' side. The cement floors were easy to clean when the animals were out strolling.

Dulary was put in a cage with Petal, the younger and friendlier of the two adults. But the first meeting between Petal and Dulary was not encouraging. Petal, interested in her new "roommate," walked toward Dulary and began sniffing her with her trunk. Dulary backed off in alarm. She might have welcomed such attention when she was new in the zoo and missed her mother, but since then she had grown attached to Ann. This big, snuffling stranger was something else.

"Dulary was just plain scared," says Ann, who watched it all. "Her ears stood straight out. She trumpeted wildly and tried to run away. But there was nowhere to run. When she realized that, she stood there and bawled.

"Finally the keeper put her in an empty cage—the last one in the house, by the way—until she could calm down and get used to being among other elephants. The keeper took special pains to soothe her and pay her attention. Bit by bit she got over her fear.

"Me? I stayed out of the picture. It wasn't my show any more. Sure, I missed that little girl. But we had to do what was best for her—and it worked."

Ann tells of another zoo baby with a similar problem. This was a lion cub named Siegfried, one of triplets born to a zoo lioness. For some reason, the mother cared for the other two cubs normally but ignored Siegfried. He was fed, therefore, from a bottle until he was old enough to take meat, and then he was put in the Children's Zoo. Young visitors could pick him up and pet him the way you would a kitten. But Siegfried grew fast, and so did his teeth and claws. When he was about ten months old, he was put back with his brothers.

"The three shared a cage in the Carnivore House," Ann says, "but Siegfried wanted no part of it. If anyone stopped to look in, the brothers usually paid no attention. But Siegfried hurried over to greet visitors and even tried to follow them away. His early days in the Children's Zoo evidently had persuaded him that he wasn't a lion at all. He was a 'people.'

"It took weeks before Siegfried would admit that he and the other two cubs were brothers after all."

During Dulary's winter of readjustment, zoo life went on all around her. Visitors came every day, but there were far fewer visitors than in summer. The weather was getting colder. Some animals were

The Impala Fountain, located in front of the new Rare Mammal House, portrays male impalas leaping over a pool of water.

no longer on view outdoors. The animal houses were heated as necessary—warmer for a hippopotamus, cooler for a zebra. Tropical birds needed constant warmth, while waterfowl could enjoy Bird Lake even

76

in freezing weather. Most animals, including elephants, were allowed out for at least a short airing except on very cold days.

When fewer visitors are in the zoo, repairs can be made more easily to buildings, enclosures and landscaping. This also is the time when the men who run the zoo look ahead and make plans. Among other things, they plan for new or improved buildings.

New buildings have become so expensive—up to $1,000,000 or more apiece—that only with city help can the Philadelphia Zoo even consider building new ones. But given the promise of funds sooner or later, each curator can think about making improvements that will better serve the needs of his collection. Which buildings need major repairs? Which can the zoo modernize by, for example, putting new floors in all the cages or installing sound-absorbent ceilings? Which buildings should be replaced?

Often major construction and repairs have to be put off for years. Take, as an example, Philadelphia's original Aviary (birdhouse), one of the original buildings when the zoo was opened in 1874. In 1882 the Aviary became the Reptile House and the birds were moved elsewhere. The Reptile House then got along with only routine repairs until 1948, when one wing was modernized. The rest of the building was modernized in 1969 and a new wing was added to provide better display space for crocodiles, alligators and big turtles. Decades may pass before there are any further important changes in the Reptile House.

One reason, besides a lack of money, that these things take time is that designing a *good* building for zoo animals isn't easy. What is involved is not just fitting cages inside walls. The needs of each kind of animal come first. Among these needs are maximum space for everyday living, exercise and breeding; objects that the animal's way of life demands (such as tree branches for small birds to perch on or scratching posts for itchy-backed buffalo); and freedom from intrusion by other animals and the public. Curators and keepers also want such things as proper lighting and heating, ways of making feeding and cleaning easier—and the best possible conditions for visitors.

Philadelphia's Elephant House meets most of these needs. An even better design is that of the new Rare Mammal House. Its main purpose is to protect species nearing extinction in the wild and to encourage them to breed in the zoo. Accordingly, cages in the Rare Mammal House are large and well lighted.

They have no bars. Instead, each is fronted by heavy glass in which electric wires are embedded. The glass keeps visitors from getting too close to the animals and wards off possible germs. The wires carry enough current so that an animal touching the glass will get a sharp (though harmless) shock and probably won't touch it again.

Thus safeguarded, the animals can live practically model lives. They are fed formulas designed to keep them in tip-top condition. They get regular exercise. And they are clean. The cage floors and walls are of tile that is easy for keepers to hose down. A special flushing system washes the floors of the bigger cages every hour and a half. Clean animals are less likely to get infections and more likely to breed. The first proof of this at the Rare Mammal House was the birth of a three-pound baby orangutan the year after the house was opened.

Other rare creatures in the building have included a mountain gorilla, ring-tailed lemurs from Madagascar, maned wolves from Argentina, red pandas from Burma, aardwolves (cousins of the hyena) from Africa and tree kangaroos from Australia. With the zoo's help, many such animals may be saved from extinction.

Buildings for mammals are, as we have seen, the

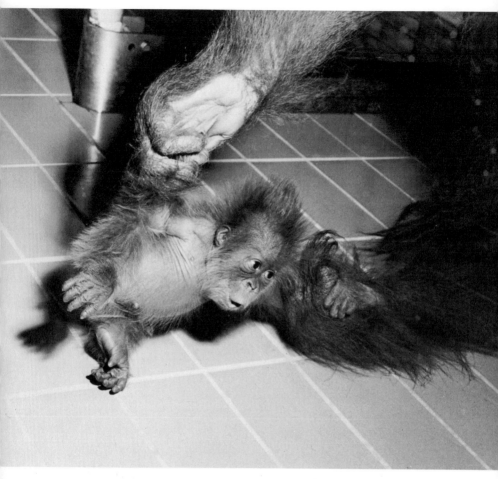

A baby female orangutan, born in the Rare Mammal House
a year after it was opened, learns to walk, with her mother's help.

concern of the Curator of Mammals. Part of his job is to keep up with new ideas at other zoos. To do this he makes regular visits to major zoos in the United States and occasionally visits zoos in Europe. He talks with other zoo men, attends their meetings and exchanges letters with them. Most of them are eager to pass along ideas that others can use.

There are also useful publications. Probably the best is the *International Zoo Yearbook*, which reports recent developments from all over the world. It is published by the Zoological Society of London (England). But a curator may get ideas from almost anywhere. Frederick Ulmer recalls an idea that struck him when a new Camel House was being planned:

"We wanted an outside enclosure where the public could watch the camels. It could have a fence to separate animals and people, but modern zoos try to do away with fences. The aim is a 'natural look.' One day I was glancing through a guidebook just mailed to us by the zoo in Munich, Germany. It had one photo of an animal enclosure with a shallow moat in front and people standing outside. It struck me as our possible answer.

"It also struck me that getting the details from Germany might take time. So I simply measured the

Sultan, a baby male camel, was born in the zoo.

moat and the people in the picture, then worked out their actual size. From that I planned our Camel House moat—three feet deep, six feet wide, with a low railing screened by a hedge on the visitors' side.

"I admit I took a gamble. A moat that small *might* not stop camels from jumping across. Or walking. When I proposed the idea to our board of directors, I got objections. So I assured them that I *knew* it would work. Finally they said OK.

"Well, you can see the result today. The camel enclosure is separated from the public just as I planned. A young camel does jump down into the moat occasionally, then back up again. Adults don't. And as visitors look across, they see the animals just a few feet away and hardly realize the moat is there.

"Guess it pays to look at pictures, doesn't it?"

8

By the end of Dulary's second winter in Philadelphia, she was too big for the Children's Zoo. She was far from full grown and she was as amiable as ever. But she weighed about 1,500 pounds and just didn't fit in with ducklings and baby llamas anymore. Somewhat reluctantly, the zoo decided that Dulary would remain in the Elephant House and it would find a replacement for the Children's Zoo.

This time the new face in the Children's Zoo belonged to a young female African elephant named Kutenga (pronounced "koo-TEN-gah"), which means "Number One." She was a gift, as Dulary had been. But she was not such a baby: she weighed 680 pounds on arrival and was estimated to be about 18 months old. Some visitors missed Dulary, but Kutenga was cute in her own right and soon grew popular.

Dulary, however, was not forgotten. She had grown used to being with the two adult elephants by now. Indeed, she undoubtedly felt as many human teen-agers do: that she had outgrown childhood and was already an adult herself. Visitors might not fully agree, for both Peggy and Petal still towered above Dulary and outweighed her several times over. Seeing the three together, many people made the natural mistake of thinking that Peggy and Petal were a breeding pair and Dulary was their child.

Ann came by often now to spend a few minutes with Dulary. Sometimes, for old times' sake, she fed Dulary the beet pulp and rolled oats (two buckets a day) that had become her steady diet, along with hay. Peggy and Petal got the same food, only more of it. Dulary was always glad to see Ann, but she didn't make a fuss when Ann went away again.

That was probably just as well, because Ann was changing jobs again. She had learned a lot about handling animals as a keeper, and now she wanted to see another side of the zoo. She decided to become a research assistant in the Penrose Research Laboratory.

Ann was making a good choice. There is nothing quite like the Philadelphia laboratory in any other American zoo. It is run by trained scientists who also teach their specialties at the University of Pennsylvania (located not far from the zoo). Together, laboratory and university have built up an exceptional amount of information about keeping animals healthy. Sometimes they work together on a case. For example, when the zoo veterinarian does a major operation on an animal patient, the university may supply a veterinarian who is an expert with anesthetics.

In most cases the vet works with only the help of the animal's keeper. One day he may set a heron's broken wing or remove an ocelot's infected kidney. The next day, he may dress a gash suffered by an elk in a fight. Operations are done right in the animal's cage or enclosure whenever possible. Some zoos have clinics or hospitals where animals are treated, but Philadelphia prefers its way.

"It can be very hard on an animal to leave the place it regards as home," a laboratory researcher explains. "Take a lemur with a cut paw. The average vet might carry it to the zoo hospital and sew up the paw as he would a dog's. A dog probably would take that all right.

"But a lemur isn't a dog. It's a primitive cousin of monkeys and apes—and man. It frightens easily. Rush it into a strange place, operate on it and you'd almost certainly send it into shock. And an animal in shock rarely survives.

"We bring care to the animal, not the other way round. You might not call that important. Believe me, it can make the difference between a live animal and a dead one."

It was to learn just such secrets of animal care that the laboratory was started, back in 1901. Very little was known then about the health and nutrition of wild animals. A zoo housed them, fed them and displayed them. They lived or they died. Most of them lived only a few years, and zoo men might guess the reasons. It took the scientific approach of laboratory workers to turn guesses into facts.

The laboratory personnel carried on long-range studies of two kinds. One was to observe closely the way animals looked and behaved under different conditions of feeding, cleanliness and so on. The other was to examine the bodies of animals that died in the zoo. That may sound unpleasant, but even close observation can't reveal what goes on inside an animal. The researcher can't ask the animal whether something hurts or whether it feels one symptom or another. He can try one treatment or another, but the animal may die anyway. So he tries to learn why and figure out something better for the next time.

That, in broad terms, is how the laboratory has done its work. It has kept records on every mammal, bird, reptile and amphibian that has died at the zoo since 1901. The total now is more than 20,000 animals. Dangerous diseases have been tracked down one by one and remedies proved by trial and error. Many ills that once beset zoo dwellers have been brought under control. The laboratory's findings are available to zoos—and veterinarians—all over the world.

No one has yet found a way to keep wild animals from hurting themselves by accident or in fights, but much has been learned about patching up the damage. Today's zoo veterinarian has drugs, anesthetics, surgical equipment—and skills—unknown in the past. He is learning more all the time.

Meanwhile, zoo animals have become more liable to certain kinds of disease (or perhaps these diseases are being identified more precisely) that, surprisingly, are often similar to those most dangerous to man. These include cancer and kidney disease, in middle age, and heart ailments of many kinds in old age. Animal researchers seek to understand and treat such things just as human doctors do. Each kind of research, animal and human, may help the other.

Humans, luckily, avoid one scourge of zoo denizens: the public. Ignorant, thoughtless or vicious people insist on acting as though wild animals could eat anything. They feed paper, plastic, wood and even metal to creatures that can no more digest such things than people can. One Philadelphia crocodile's stomach was examined after the animal died. It contained, among other tidbits, a penny and a false tooth.

Adds a Penrose researcher: "More of our animals die just after summer weekends than at any other time. Pressure from all those visitors has to be a factor. And it's known that stresses of one kind or another help bring on heart disease in everything from chickens to tigers."

Still, Philadelphia's concern with disease control and proper feeding has paid off in many ways. One is the ripe old age many of its animals have been reaching. Some of them have set world records. Among others, a camel chalked up 28 years in the zoo; a swan, 29; a gibbon, 31, a vulture, 34; a hippo, 36; a stork, 39, a flamingo, 44; a snapping turtle (the champion so far), 58. Philadelphia also is credited with old-age records for such rarities as a monkey called a red uakari (8), a big-headed rodent called a pacarana (9), a tiny, huge-eared fox called a fennec (10½) and a gentle little deer called a Reeve's muntjac (16).

In addition, until 1961 Philadelphia had the world's oldest captive gorilla, a famous male named Bamboo. When he died he had been a zoo inhabi-

Massa, the world's oldest captive gorilla, is 39 years old.

tant for 33 years. A second gorilla, Massa, has since broken Bamboo's record. As this book is written, Massa is 39 years old. His black hair is turning silver, but he still is full of life and seems to know that he is considered something special.

Just how special could be seen one day when his keeper noted a swelling in Massa's left nostril. It might or might not be serious, but the zoo veterinarian wanted to take no chances. He decreed a thorough examination. That meant Massa would have to be given a drug to make him unconscious. The staff assembled for this rare occasion included two scientists from the laboratory, three university veterinarians and a human eye, ear, nose and throat specialist from the university as well.

Gorillas are smart and suspicious, so the doctors tricked Massa: they gave him orange juice with an anesthetic in it. Moments later he lay unconscious on the floor of his cage.

The big ape, they found, had an abscess in his left cheek. It was full of pus and probably quite painful. The zoo veterinarian broke into it so that the pus could drain away. While Massa was unconscious, other tests were performed and blood samples were taken for analysis in the laboratory.

The next day Massa was up and around, happy

as always when people peered in through the glass of his cage. Many of them had read in the newspapers about his condition and were relieved that he looked so fine. He peered back at them, grunted, threw wisps of hay over his head and generally behaved as though he had never had an operation. The veterinarian, though, was afraid he might develop an infection and prescribed antibiotic pills—twelve a day.

The job of giving Massa his medicine fell to Ann, who in her new laboratory job had become friendly with the gorilla. She says it wasn't easy:

"I wanted to fool him by putting the pills into sections of banana. He was so busy showing off to visitors that he wouldn't eat. Then he took some banana, spotted the strange little lump in it and spat the whole thing out. Pretty soon we had pills all over the place, but none in Massa.

"Later I tried again. I put pills into everything he likes—grapes, meat, oranges, more bananas. This time he was hungrier. He spotted some but took others, and finally the job was done.

"No, the infection never did develop. If it had, I'm sure the vet would have thought of something else."

With every zoo animal, of course, there comes a

time when "something else" no longer works. If the animal becomes too old to feed itself, or develops a disease that can't be cured, or has an accident that cripples it forever, the zoo must make a decision.

"If the animal is in pain," a Philadelphia scientist says, "we help if we can. If it reaches the point where we can't help, the only answer is euthanasia."

Euthanasia means mercy killing. The zoo uses a drug called sodium pentobarbital. It is painless. The animal is dead within a few seconds. Compared with the way most animals die in the wild, this is a merciful way of killing indeed.

9

In her new home at the Elephant House Dulary kept growing, up to and past the one-ton mark. Kutenga kept growing too. Like Dulary, she became too big for the Children's Zoo after two seasons. She too had to move into the Elephant House, making way for yet another replacement.

Kutenga was put in with Dulary, and at once a new problem came up. The African elephant, though younger and smaller than Dulary, had a bossy streak. She began butting Dulary almost as soon as they were together, and kept it up. When the keeper brought their hay, Kutenga tried to keep Dulary away from it. Outside, when peanuts were offered Dulary, Kutenga moved in and grabbed them. It wasn't fair, and one day Dulary said so.

"They had what you might call an argument," Ann says, smiling. "I guess Dulary told Kutenga to cut it out. There was some shoving and snorting. Dulary was bigger, and Kutenga couldn't push her around unless Dulary let her.

**Dulary, now a young adult, enjoys a visit
from her good friend Ann Lewis.**

"I think Kutenga got the message. Anyway, the butting stopped."

So peace and quiet settled over the Elephant House. For the two youngsters life was good. They had plenty to eat, lots of attention, a considerate keeper, expert medical care if it was needed. There was scant reason to miss the existence they might have led elsewhere. Life in the wild would have been more exciting, but a lot more dangerous. Here they would be safe and comfortable. Someday Dulary might even break the zoo's record age for an Asiatic elephant—38 years in captivity.